Using Spiritual Rescue Technology

BOOK 2 OF THE SRT SERIES

Second
Edition

Harness the Power of

Your Spiritual Connections

By David St. Lawrence

Text copyright ©2015 David St. Lawrence

All Rights Reserved

TABLE OF CONTENTS

TABLE OF CONTENTS iii
INTRODUCTION 1
HOW TO USE THIS BOOK 5
GENERAL PREPARATIONS 8
    1. Preparing for an SRT Counseling Session 9
    2. Choosing a Counseling Partner 12
    3. Establishing Trust with Your partner 16
    4. Handling Mistakes Made in Session 21
RUNNING A SPIRITUAL RESCUE TECHNOLOGY SESSION 24
    Overview 24
    2. What Topics Do You Take Up First? 26
    3. Handling Entities Who Won't Communicate 29
    4. Overcoming Your Personal Barriers to Handling Entities 32
    5. Handling Clusters 33
    6. Entities With Entities Attached to Them 36
    7. Handling Someone Who Can't Perceive Entities 40

Table of Contents

8. Handling Someone Who is Possessed by Entities 43

9. Handling Someone Who Has been harmed by Other Spiritual Practices 46

10. Handling Disturbed Animals 48

11. Handling Situations You Can't Share with Anyone 51

12. Handling Entities Who Interrupt Sessions 54

13. A Powerful Undercut for SRT Processing on New People or to Handle Unusual Situations 57

EXAMPLES OF SPECIFIC SESSION TOPICS 61

1. Taking Up What You Observe First 61

2. Difficulty in Comprehending Something Important 66

3. Distractions Affecting Your Ability to Get Things Done 71

4. Cravings for Anything 76

6. Aversions 87

7. Being Possessed by Recently Deceased Entities 90

Table of Contents

    8. Fear of Closeness to a Sexual or Marital Partner 97

    9. Handling a Being Who Thinks He is You ... 102

ADDITIONAL LIST OF TOPICS TO CHECK 108

    1. Inappropriate or Recurring Emotional Reactions, Moods or Fears 108

    2. Distractions 110

    3. Compulsions 111

    4. Aversions 114

    5. Physical Sensations/Pains 115

    6. Inexplicable Events, Trends or Behavior in Self or Others 115

    7. Warnings/Messages 117

    8. Physical Universe Manifestations 119

    Additional Notes 119

EXTENDED SPIRITUAL RESCUE TECHNOLOGY 122

    1. Use of Processes and Lists Developed by Others 124

    2. Working with Spiritual Teammates 125

SPIRITUAL COUNSELOR'S CODE 128

ACKNOWLEDGMENTS 131

Table of Contents

ABOUT THE AUTHOR.. 132

INTRODUCTION

This second book of the Spiritual Rescue Technology series is designed for the person who wishes to harness the power of their spiritual connections so that they can bring about spectacular changes in their abilities to control their destinies.

We are surrounded by innumerable spiritual beings (entities) and our lives and fortunes depend on our ability to help spiritually damaged entities and on our ability to recruit and motivate entities who wish to be our spiritual teammates.

Our research has shown us that it is almost impossible to increase our own ability while excluding other beings in the process. Like it or not, we are accompanied through life by thousands of spiritual entities and our success in life and our physical well-being is directly proportional to the percentage of these entities who are supporting us at any moment.

This book will enable a person to train himself or herself to communicate effectively with entities on their own or with a partner and make significant changes in their lives and fortunes.

Introduction

We know this can be done because there have been many people have started using Spiritual Rescue Technology (SRT) after reading about it on the original http://spiritual-rescue-technology.com/ website or on the http://srtforum.info website. They contacted us only when they needed more information than they could find on the original sites.

This book is designed for use by someone who has already read and understood the first book in the series, *Introducing Spiritual Rescue Technology.* You can consider this book to be a "How To" book on dealing with spiritual beings in trouble, whereas the first book is a "What Is" book covering the background and theory of Spiritual Rescue Technology. If you have not read the first book, you will probably not be able to apply the material in this book.

This book contains detailed procedures for handling many different situations that people find themselves in because of upset spiritual beings. We are constantly surrounded by spiritual beings or entities who have a direct effect on our feelings and our actions, but fortunately most of these entities are benign and even helpful.

Introduction

When you are surrounded by helpful entities, life seems to go well and problems are easily handled. You will definitely feel that fortune is favoring you. Answers to problems often seem to come to you out of thin air.

When you have upset entities surrounding you, life becomes much more difficult, you can have serious mood swings, you will find yourself making mistakes, and you may even be plagued with unresolvable fears. You may find it very difficult to be creative, and life can even seem hopeless as that is what the entities are feeling.

This book will give you the tools for helping upset entities become happy and productive again and to recruit them to help you if you wish.

In order to make this possible, this book includes many specific session reports from those who have run SRT sessions on themselves and on others so you can see how they have handled situations you will encounter when using SRT to help entities.

If you find that you are having difficulty getting the results you want, you are invited to join the SRT forum at http://srtforum.info. There you will find helpful people who can direct you to the

Introduction

information or services you need to get the full benefits of using SRT in your life.

Our research has shown us that it is almost impossible to increase our own ability while excluding other beings in the process. Like it or not, we are accompanied through life by thousands of spiritual entities and our success in life and our physical well-being is directly proportional to the percentage of these entities who are supporting us at any moment.

HOW TO USE THIS BOOK

You might wish to read this book from end to end as a first step. This will give you a useful overview of the tools available to you and the situations you will encounter when using Spiritual Rescue Technology (SRT) on yourself or your partner.

Once you have an idea of the scope of this book, you will probably find the Table of Contents to be your most useful tool for using the data in this book, as it provides links to every session topic and to every step of your preparations for an SRT session.

Special Note:

If you can't find what you want in the Table of Contents, you can always use the Search function to look up a word or key phrase that describes what you are seeking.

SRT sessions are relaxed communications between you, your counseling partner, and the entities who are being rescued. Therefore, you should feel free to stop and look up a reference if you encounter something in session that you have never experienced before. You, your partner, and the entities involved will be better off understanding what is going on and knowing that it has been handled successfully before.

You will encounter an enormous range of entities, all the way from dead relatives, disembodied spirits and demons, to Greek Gods and legendary historical figures. All entities are immortal, as you and I are, so they have an enormous range of experiences which have occurred over unimaginably long periods of time. Be prepared to experience anything in your SRT sessions and focus on helping the entities resolve whatever problem they are still stuck in.

Your ability to understand what the entity is trying to communicate is critical to your success in using SRT. Take whatever identity the entity presents without question or evaluation and stick with the standard SRT process.

If you do this, you will be surprised how easily you are able to handle the entity's problem whether he presents himself as a Reptilian or any other alien species. Beings have worn MANY different bodies during their past lives. You just take what they give you and help them with SRT.

If you know that entities exist in hundreds of different forms and that they all represent attempts at solving problems that could not be handled otherwise, you will find that you can be compassionate and can help them resolve the situations that started them off on a long and ultimately self-destructive existence.

All entities are immortal, as are you and I, so they have an enormous range of experiences which have occurred over unimaginably long periods of time. Be prepared to experience anything in your SRT sessions.

GENERAL PREPARATIONS

You should read and understand this section before attempting any extended Spiritual Rescue Technology sessions. These are hard-won practical suggestions for producing consistently satisfactory sessions by yourself or with a partner. Yes, you can skip over this section and get to work, but sooner or later, you may run into problems which can easily be avoided if you read this section and get all of your questions answered first.

When you understand the philosophy of SRT—which is to care for spiritual beings you will be rescuing from various past incidents—you will find it easy to apply the process steps, as they fall in a natural order that is easy to remember, and you will produce new spiritual friends with every session.

A well-executed SRT session is as effortless as a conversation can be with interesting people. Done correctly, you will be freeing some spiritual beings from ages of torment, and you will earn their trust while doing it. You will also learn about a great deal of history which never made it into the history books. Ever.

If you encounter words you do not understand, you should open *Introducing Spiritual Rescue*

Technology again and search for the word you need defined.

For best results, read this section and get all of your questions answered before starting your first session.

1. Preparing for an SRT Counseling Session

Communicating with entities is a skill that takes practice and concentration and a full understanding of entities as living beings.

Ideally, you should relax yourself before session by some form of meditation or mental exercise that brings you calmly into present time. Let go of any concerns or distractions and JUST BE THERE to communicate effectively with the entities you are trying to help.

If you have ever received "help" from someone who had their attention on other things, you will know how unsatisfactory that kind of help can be. When you are running an SRT session, you should have all of your attention on the beings you are communicating with and on your partner in order to have a successful session.

Running a Spiritual Rescue Technology Session

Now, if you are having a session because some entity is frantically yammering at you to get your attention, you can make the preparation very short indeed because you are already getting an urgent communication, and you should respond promptly and let the entity know you are willing to help him.

Being there and being willing to communicate is the first step. The second step is recognizing that you are communicating with someone who is alive and aware, even though he may not have a body at the current time.

You will know you are fully prepared to run SRT when you are reaching out to entities as potential friends and partners, even though they may seem hostile or indifferent at first.

Entities are alive and you can get more spiritual improvement than you can imagine by rescuing them and putting them to work on projects that interest them. You will have realizations and they will have realizations.

You will find that the SRT process steps will allow you to change fixed considerations, prejudices, viewpoints, and ideas about how to survive that have been in place for many lifetimes. This ability to change the considerations of other beings can open the door to futures you were never able to envision before.

If you find you cannot consider entities as potential friends and partners, you may be surrounded by entities who are so suspicious, hopeless, or insane that they are preventing you from achieving a state of calm certainty and a willingness to help others.

If this is the case, you should arrange to receive SRT sessions from a student counselor or professional SRT counselor until you are able to successfully handle entities on your own.

People have been successfully processed by a partner even when they have *never* been successful at contacting entities by themselves in a solo session.

2. Choosing a Counseling Partner

When you partner with someone for SRT sessions, one of you is the client and the other takes the role of the SRT counselor. You should swap roles every few sessions so that both of you get practice as a counselor and as a client. It is a valuable experience being a client because you will soon understand the absolute necessity of following the SRT Counselor's Code, and you will become a better counselor when it is your turn to help someone else.

A successful SRT session should be a relaxed conversation with your entities, so your counseling partner should be someone who makes it easy for you to communicate and does not inhibit or interfere with your communication in any way.

Your partner should be someone you are comfortable with, and that is more important than having a partner who is highly trained but who is not necessarily easy to work with.

You will be swapping roles frequently so your partner should also be comfortable with you running SRT processes on him.

 A successful SRT session should be a relaxed conversation with your entities, so your counseling partner should be someone who makes it easy for you to communicate and does not inhibit or interfere with your communication in any way.

One of the other things that comes come up in partnered sessions is that you will occasionally have to correct your partner or vice versa when one of you mishandles a communication or tries to tell the person who is being the client in the session what to think about something.

Telling a client what to think is evaluation and is very destructive, because the client is saying what he perceives to be the truth and you are basically telling him that this is not right or should not be said.

Advising someone is evaluation, and you should never advise your partner about anything he says or discovers. You should just acknowledge what he says and get him to continue rescuing beings from incidents.

When you are a client and your partner is running the session, you are expected to let your partner know when he has violated the SRT Counselor's Code. It is cruel to let him or her go on violating some part of the Counselor's Code when you can tactfully indicate his error and help him to be a better counselor.

If you cannot get your partner to follow the SRT Counselor's Code, you should end off on your partnership as your sessions will only worsen conditions instead of improving them.

If you want to receive SRT sessions but are not sufficiently trained to give sessions to a partner, then you should ask for some free student counseling on the SRT forum at http://srtforum.info.

We have a growing number of student counselors who are training to be full-time professional counselors, and these students need to get a lot of experience delivering SRT sessions until they are so proficient and comfortable with this technology that they can handle anything that comes their way.

You may find that more than one person wishes to partner with you. The best way to handle this is for three or four of you to give sessions to each other on a round-robin basis so you all can have frequent sessions on some sort of regular schedule.

You will find that your knowledge of SRT grows very rapidly when you are delivering sessions to someone else. If you are delivering sessions and receiving sessions, you will get the best of all both worlds, since you are getting spiritual benefit and you are learning how to help others more or less at the same time.

The final benefit of partnering on SRT is that two people working together will find it easier to spot entities and clusters that are attempting to hide or remain invisible to a person who is working alone.

It is almost impossible when working alone to handle entities who make you feel apathetic, hopeless, or suicidal. Their emotions can overpower yours and make you unable to approach them in a caring manner to help them.

If you have difficulty communicating with entities when soloing on SRT, you should find a counseling partner who is more cheerful and optimistic than you are, or get counseling from a student SRT counselor or a professional SRT counselor.

3. Establishing Trust with Your partner

A professional SRT counselor should have trained himself/herself to be trustworthy under all conditions. A student SRT counselor can be very trustworthy under most conditions, while a partner may still have difficulty following the SRT Counselor's Code under certain circumstances.

So, it is up to you to satisfy yourself that you feel comfortable with any partner, student, or counselor before you make arrangements for a series of sessions. You should feel free to determine if the personal chemistry between the two of you makes you feel safe about confiding in a partner, student, or SRT professional.

This is no different from deciding whether a medical practitioner is right for you. Some very skillful practitioners can have personality quirks that make them unsuitable for you or your family members.

Running a Spiritual Rescue Technology Session

You should choose a partner who understands you and who does not try to tell you what to think in session. It is really important in SRT for your partner to respond properly when you are trying to describe some situation that you do not fully understand. It is a huge relief when your partner lets you know that he understands what you are trying to describe, without telling you what he sees or explaining things to you.

Often, he can do this by asking the right question.

Example: You try to describe an incident where you are put in a box of some sort and are whirled around for a long time and the dizziness never ends.

If your partner stares at you in an uncomprehending silence, you have a serious problem.

If your partner gently asks about the incident, you will experience relief and the entire situation may open up like some Origami figure.

Your counseling partner will be able to see things you cannot see if he is truly in communication with you. The telepathic bond between the two of you will reveal to him what you are looking at and will also let him see what entities are thinking about while you are trying to help them.

During session, you are asking questions of entities and seeking to receive answers while your counseling partner will be observing both sides of the conversation. He will also be picking up considerations and intentions that are not being voiced.

If he leaves you alone while you are still looking for answers and lets you work away until you either come up dry or find answers, he is a gem of a partner.

If he interrupts you while you are looking inward for answers to more questions, he is a hindrance and you need to let him know he is interrupting you.

 A good counseling partner lets you look as long as you wish and will ask a new question only when it appears that you are stumped.

As you work together, you and your partner will learn each other's speed of thought, and you will find that sessions flow very smoothly with no halts or upsets. In addition, if you and your partner are truly in synch, you will know when your partner has another question for you, and you will pick it out of his mind and use it yourself in the session. This is not an interruption—it is like having someone hold out a cue card for you in the middle of the process.

Spending time talking with a partner before you have any session together is time well spent. You should probably discuss the SRT Counselor's Code with your partner and see if he has any considerations about it—including what parts of the Code he considers most important.

You may even find that your partner does very well on certain things, but has differences of opinions about other aspects of spiritual activity.

If this is the case, use this partner for those things you both agree on and find another partner to work with on the topics that the first partner didn't view in the same way that you do.

For example: I have found that some people have a tendency to worship entities who present themselves as SATAN, LUCIFER, YAHWEH, or any of the Host of Angels.

It makes it impossible for them to actually help these beings since they consider the beings to be from a higher plane and therefore to be exempt from SRT handlings.

At other times, groups of beings have presented themselves as the "Galactic Council for Peace and Understanding", and this has so completely overawed the person that they cannot maintain the personal presence necessary to control and run the session.

These "overawed" people have adopted SRT to receive guidance from a higher plane, and we have not yet discovered any entities who fall into this category, so if your partner has a mission of this type, do not try to correct him in session. Simply end off comfortably and let him decide on his own if he wishes to continue SRT processing.

 *SRT processing has nothing to do with finding someone to worship—it is a spiritual tool to set entities free.*

4. Handling Mistakes Made in Session

There are times when you will ask a question or say something that upsets your entities or upsets your partner and his entities. If you do not know your SRT Counselor's Code forward and backward, this will almost certainly happen more often than it should.

The Counselor's Code is not there as an afterthought. It contains all of the things that could possibly stop a session from producing results, and if you do not follow it, you are not using SRT correctly. You might as well be using Voodoo or hypnotism, and your clients and your entities will come to hate you and shut off communication with you.

Spiritual Rescue Technology is based on trust between the person and the entities he is helping.

When you are partnering with another person, the trust is a three-way agreement between the two partners and the entities being helped.

Running a Spiritual Rescue Technology Session

ANY COMMENT about what the partner or his entities have said can act as evaluation, and this will shatter the trust between the parties since it is an effort to correct or change the value of something that was said in session.

Examples of wrong and right handlings:

Someone says, "I pushed them under the water and drowned them."

Wrong: "Didn't that make you feel bad?"

Wrong: "Wow! That sounds weird!"

Wrong: "I'm sure you didn't mean it."

Wrong: "How awful!"

Right: "What happened just before that?"

Right: "Is there anything else you did there?"

Right: "OK! Why was it necessary to drown them?"

Right: "How did you justify that?"

If you find you have made a comment instead of acknowledging the person's statement and it has upset the person, you will need to apologize and take responsibility for your mistake.

Do not explain why you made the mistake—just say you should not have said what you did as since it is a violation of the Counselor's Code.

There are some schools of thought that feel that a counselor or a therapist or a doctor should never apologize, but you will find that a sincere apology will mend the upset, and any other course of action will eventually lose you a client.

You will have to mend your relationships with the entities, or the session will grind to a halt and you will end up talking to yourself with nobody responding.

You will need to apologize for ignoring your entities in order for conversation to resume. If you are sincere and do not repeat the mistake, you will find that most entities are quite forgiving.

There are some schools of thought that feel that a counselor or a therapist or a doctor should never apologize for a mistake, but you will find that a sincere apology will mend the upset, and any other course of action will eventually lose you a client.

RUNNING A SPIRITUAL RESCUE TECHNOLOGY SESSION

Overview

An SRT session can be initiated simply by noticing that the person is stuck in an undesired mood or attitude and asking him, "Where is that mood or attitude located?" and having him spot that the mood or attitude is external to him and is being generated by someone else.

Once the person spots that he is dealing with something external to himself, you can ask him such questions as, "How big is the area where this feeling originates? Or, what color does it appear to be?"

Once the person is communicating with the area, you can get the person to tell you if there is one entity or many and how long it has been with him. You can then get the entity to identify the incident which caused them to lose their last body or which made them into a cluster.

Once the incident is identified and described by the entities, you can ask questions designed to get the entity to discover what part he played in causing himself to be involved in the incident.

There will always be some action or lack of action that caused the being to experience the incident.

When you find it, you need to get the reasons the being caused the incident or failed to prevent the incident from happening.

You simply ask how did he justify doing or not doing what was required. When you get all of his justifications, he will realize how he caused himself to be involved and he will no longer be stuck in the incident or its aftermath. He will be ready to create a new life for himself and move on to a new game.

Here is a brief checklist of things to do when the entities are unstuck from the incident:

1. Make sure they have no further attention on the incident that was handled.

2. Let them know they are immortal and what that means to them.

3. Make sure they are ready to create a new future for themselves.

4. Answer any questions they may have.

5. Let them know if you wish to recruit them for future projects.

6. Get them oriented to the planet as it is today by sending them on a tour of appropriate places.

Most of your encounters with entities will go swiftly and easily, but I have included some tips for the more challenging situations.

2. What Topics Do You Take Up First?

For several years, I merely asked the client what he had his attention on, and we took up what indicated most. This worked quite well, but I would occasionally find we had missed a significant area of upset because the client was pursuing things that were of interest to him without regard to how it affected his financial or family survival.

This might come up after months of SRT counseling when the client would mention that he could not afford more counseling until he had a job or until his business improved. Since the whole purpose in delivering SRT to this person was to improve his opportunities in life, I decided to ask each new client about the areas of his life that were important to his personal survival and prosperity.

It was quite easy to spot the areas of a client's life that were in trouble because he would often have difficulty looking at these areas and talking about them. The client had often created methods of compensating for these problem areas and would interject dismissive statements about any problem connected with these areas. This mechanism was an indication that his entities were speaking for him, and this was usually the root of his problem.

There would be an area of his life or his business which was not going well, and he would have entities finding all sorts of excuses for him to avoid solving the existing problem. Entities are masters of distraction and when the client would sit down to pay his bills, the entities would create in the client an urgent need to check on his email or to feed the dog. Two hours later, he would be reading Facebook and the bills would not have been paid.

I would not do a lengthy search for problem areas. Instead, I would get him to talk about his finances until he identified a problem in that area that really indicated to him. Or, if the problem seemed to be in the area of relationships, I would get the client to discuss any difficulties he was having with other people until he could identify something that made him get really emotional about his dealings with people.

Once we located a hot area, we would then search for evidence of entity interference or false data or things being hidden about the area.

Sometimes, we would find evidence of all three. We would take up the personal acts that were causing damage and had been hidden, and then expand to see if entities were behind these contra-survival actions.

If we came to false data where the client was saying and relying on things that were obviously not true, we would do a light process in which we would ask where the information came from and what did the person look like when saying it to the client.

Starting each session by checking on the state of the client's business or personal relationships, we kept cleaning up those areas of the client's life which would contribute most to his prosperity and happiness.

When clients finally realized that SRT could actually improve the quality of their lives and not just make them feel better, they developed a much more professional attitude toward their SRT processing.

Running SRT on the big problem areas of their lives freed up enough attention so that they could take up minor issues without feeling guilty. These minor issues would often be taken up in session after the areas of heavy upset were handled.

When clients finally realized that SRT could actually improve the quality of their lives and not just make them feel better, they developed a much more professional attitude toward their SRT processing.

3. Handling Entities Who Won't Communicate

If you ask an entity a question telepathically and they do not respond, it can be quite frustrating. There are several solutions to this problem and you should check them out in the following order:

- Do you really care about this entity and want to make it a friend or set it free to create a new future? If not, you need to address why you cannot view the entity as a potential friend. You will probably need help from an experienced SRT student for this.

- You should not attempt to handle entities until you are calm and completely willing to engage them in conversation and help them create a new future. If you still have difficulty considering these entities as living beings with intelligence and a sense of humor, go back and repeat the previous step.

There are some people who find it very hard to recognize that spiritual entities are actually people without bodies. These people generally need help from a trained SRT practitioner in finding the source of their resistance to recognizing entities as being alive and intelligent. This resistance usually comes from indoctrination in some religious practice which forbids talking to spirits or demons.

- Ask the entity if it is OK for you to help him. You will generally get an answer and if he says no, you should ask if you or anyone else has failed to help him. Once he starts talking about this failed help, you can generally get him to keep talking to you until he begins to open up and answer questions about the incident he still has his attention on.

- If he is still reluctant to communicate, you should ask him if you have done anything to harm him. Let him discuss any grievance he has with you and take responsibility for causing the upset. If you try to defend yourself or make him wrong for being upset with you, you will make no progress and he may shut down completely.

- Once you get into good communication with an entity, do not mess up the communication flow by lecturing him or thinking less of the entity for what he has done. You are there to listen and to get him to view what has happened to him and why he did it—not to get him to change his ways or to scold him for what he has done. You ask questions and you acknowledge his answers until he discovers something about his past which sets him free forever from his earlier mistakes.

- If you make a mistake and evaluate for the entity or tell him what he did was wrong, you will have to work very hard to regain his confidence, and it this may require assistance from another SRT practitioner. If you take what the entity says and acknowledge it, you will be safe and the session will go well.

4. Overcoming Your Personal Barriers to Handling Entities

If you spot that you have personal barriers to working with entities and helping them solve their problems, you should ask for help from a student SRT counselor or a professional. This is not something you will be able to address on your own as it is very hard to spot the source, and it may be made worse by the presence of entities who do not want you to handle anyone or change things.

If you have personal barriers to thinking of entities as potential friends, you will still be able to enjoy the benefits of SRT processing, but you should have SRT delivered to you by someone else who cares about entities and can coach you through the steps of handling entities and clusters.

Eventually, you will discover the source of your difficulty and may be able to run SRT on your own as a solo action. Working with spiritual entities is not something you generally learn in school or in life, so it is not surprising that you may need some help getting started.

Once you overcome your barriers to communicating with and helping spiritual entities, you should be able to help others who encounter this problem.

5. Handling Clusters

A cluster is a group of spiritual beings who have experienced some really traumatic incident and who are still fixated on that experience. What happens is that some disaster strikes a group and everyone in the group is overwhelmed and killed while being aware that there are others sharing the traumatic experience.

There is usually an incomplete action or feeling of betrayal which leaves the entities stuck in that moment in time.

When you contact a cluster, you will find that the beings in the cluster do not see themselves as individuals but as a single unit that is completely overwhelmed by a shared experience. You will find it seems to them that time stopped at that horrific moment, and they think they are still IN that moment. These moments of overwhelm can range from being hit by an explosion, to dying in a gas chamber with others, to going down on a sinking ship. Cluster-making incidents can be very, very old or very recent, and they will give you a perspective on past lives like nothing else can.

 ***A cluster is a group of spiritual beings who have experienced some really traumatic incident and who are still fixated on that experience.***

Here are just a few of the clusters my clients have encountered in SRT sessions:

- A group of boys who died in a car crash in Fremont, CA

- A family who died in the atomic bomb blast at Hiroshima

- A group of Orthodox Jews who died in a concentration camp gas chamber

- A drunken crew who died in a spaceship crash a very long time ago

- A group of beings who were herded up and processed in an implant station which used extreme torture and hypnosis

- A group who died on the Titanic

- Boys who died from an overdose of drugs

- A group of warriors who were poisoned at a feast celebrating the cessation of hostilities

- Soldiers killed in battle because of betrayals by their officers

- A group of people who died as a result of an orgy that got out of control

- A planet full of people whose planet was sucked into a black hole (The entire incident took 12 hours.)

When you contact a cluster, you generally ask how many entities are in the cluster because this will give them a sense of their individual existence and will give you an idea of the magnitude of the disaster that overwhelmed them.

You then try to get them to identify the incident and describe what occurred until they begin to see themselves as separate individuals instead of a group identity. You may have to ask who is willing to speak for the cluster if you get no response when asking questions.

Finally, you get them to tell what warnings they ignored or what actions they took that precipitated the disaster. You may have to get them to give you the excuses they used or the justifications they had for not taking action to avert the disaster.

The cluster will break up and dissipate when the individual members finally recognize their responsibility for being in the incident.

Clusters can be composed of multiple clusters which have accumulated many disastrous incidents over time. The handling is much the same. You take the most recent incident and the cluster breaks down into separate beings and remaining clusters. You take up the next available incident and repeat the process used on the first.

Some clusters are so big and so dense that handling them completely may take weeks or months. You stop whenever there is a major release point and celebrate that victory, leaving the remaining cluster fragments for another day.

6. Entities With Entities Attached to Them

We who have bodies have entities surrounding us and attached to us for various reasons, and these entities affect us constantly unless we have applied

SRT and handled them to the point where they are contributing to us as our spiritual teammates.

The spiritual entities we deal with in sessions may have additional entities and clusters associated with them, but the only time you should have to deal with this situation is when the entity balks or stalls during the handling cycle. Otherwise the entity can be handled as a single being with good results.

Normally, once you encounter an entity and strike up a conversation with him, you can locate the incident he is fixated on and easily get him to the point where he recognizes that he caused the incident through his own action or inaction.

Sometimes, however, the spiritual entity keeps justifying his actions by making others wrong or keeps making you wrong for attempting to help him, or he really has no idea why he committed the actions he did. He is not taking, or cannot take, responsibility for his actions. This is an indication that he was and still is being controlled by other entities and clusters.

As soon as you ask if he has other entities or clusters in his space, he will show signs of relief and will begin to be much more cooperative. If he does not feel he has entities or clusters controlling him, you should ask if he is connected to someone or something elsewhere. It will usually be other entities, clusters or machinery located at some incredibly distant location.

These other entities and clusters may be a small isolated group connected with one incident, or they may be an entire array of entities organized in multiple levels of command and control or even a huge distributed network of beings engaged in a long-term campaign of some sort.

You may even encounter a "body in pawn" situation where the being has been convinced that he has a body being kept somewhere for him and that he has to return to it whenever he dies during a mission.

To handle any of these various situations, you merely get in communication with the other entities or clusters, etc., and handle them with the usual SRT questions. You will find that in almost all cases, these entities are still operating on some old orders from an ancient authoritarian regime or civilization that disappeared ages ago.

Almost all seem to have been sent on missions to accomplish some task or to keep track of someone, and they just kept on doing that job forever and ever.

Once you get in communication with these entities and ask about the terms of their employment and duration of service, they begin to wake up and become interested in getting on with their lives as individuals.

You do not have to go on an endless handling of every entity everywhere. You just have to do enough to get most of them unstuck from the incidents and missions they are fixated on and then get them willing to get on with their lives.

You need to make sure that you end the session by handling the first spiritual entity you encountered in the session.

When he is no longer concerned with the entities he has been carrying around, you are ready to complete his handling and get him oriented to life on Earth.

You do not have to go on an endless handling of every entity everywhere. You just have to do enough to get most of them unstuck from the incidents and missions they are fixated on and then get them willing to get on with their lives.

7. Handling Someone Who Can't Perceive Entities

We have discovered from our years of counseling sessions that at least 70% of the people we encounter can perceive entities with less than an hour of running SRT on them. The other 30% fall in several categories.

There are those who have been told not to communicate with spirits at the risk of eternal damnation. They will resolutely ignore any spiritual activity and focus their attention on blocking spiritual communication with prayer or a mantra of some sort.

Others choose to ignore voices in their heads and thoughts that might not be theirs. They fear that awareness of spiritual entities might make them seem odd or unacceptable in polite society.

Finally, there are those whose minds are closed to any counseling of any kind.

All of these can be reached with SRT using processes that act on entities independently of the person who is ignoring these entities.

 Running SRT on a third person's entities is a procedure that is used whenever the third person is unable to confront communicating with entities. Almost any student or practitioner of SRT can communicate with entities connected to someone else.

This is best done by a practitioner working with a person who knows the third person well. The third person might be a religious type who will not allow himself to speak about or to spirits.

The third person might be a child or someone who is so ill that he cannot be counseled directly.

Someone suffering from Alzheimer's may be unable to speak, but their entities can be contacted and helped so that the patient gets spiritual and physical relief.

Sometimes a family member may oppose the use of SRT procedures and insist on being left alone even while demonstrating the adverse effects of entity possession.

Contacting their entities will quickly reveal the source of their upsets and mental difficulties. These entities will be found to welcome communication because they have been prevented from communicating and will have a lot of pent up emotion which they were not able to discharge.

The person may be resolutely ignoring every effort by their entities to communicate, but the entities will be eager for someone to acknowledge them and recognize that they exist.

The way third party entities are handled is simplicity itself. The practitioner and the client look at the third person's space and observe any clusters or entities that are disturbed and handle them in the same fashion as entities anywhere else.

You should definitely get the entities agreement to be helped before beginning any effort at running SRT. Caring communication is the key to helping entities and this is especially true when you are helping entities that are not your own.

The person may be resolutely suppressing every effort by their entities to communicate, but the entities will be eager for someone to acknowledge them and recognize that they exist.

8. Handling Someone Who is Possessed by Entities

Some people are so sensitive to other spiritual beings that they will pick up entities just by walking through a hospital or by walking near the site of a recent accident. These people will change personality after encountering disembodied spirits, and you will see them jump from one personality to another while talking to you.

They often hold conversations with these entities for long periods of time, and the conversations may be long and quite involved. These conversations with invisible beings can be quite disturbing to friends and family. In addition, the number of entities striving to get the attention of these people can make it very difficult for you to carry on a conversation with them as they keep interrupting themselves.

Someone like this may be too distracted to receive SRT directly. There is a solution and that is for a professional SRT practitioner to run SRT on the entities of this person with the assistance of a family member or friend who knows them well.

This can be done without directly involving the possessed person in the SRT session. The practitioner and the family member address the entities of the disturbed person directly and do not involve the disturbed person in the process. The disturbed person will show signs of relief as the troublesome entities are handled one by one.

It is possible to counsel a possessed person but it takes a great deal of patience and a thorough knowledge of entity behavior plus a willingness to negotiate with the various beings that are running the possessed individual.

I have been working with one possessed individual for several months and he, in his own words, has come out of his "insanity" and is now able to maintain a normal conversation for several days at a time.

The basic approach in this case is to open communication with whoever is running the person and to indicate that I wish to converse with the person owning the body. Sometimes the being "on duty" is willing to talk to me and I run SRT on him until he moves off. Usually, the being "disappears" as soon as I ask him questions and another being or the person himself responds.

I make it clear that I wish to talk to the person himself and persist until I get in communication with him.

This usually results in a few minutes of lucid communication with the possessed person during each session. This seems like a very slow procedure but the person's parents are extremely happy with the changes they notice in their child's behavior.

They have employed psychiatrists and institutional confinement for many years with no result. The power of SRT has produced an apparent return to normality merely through the action of communicating rationally with entities and the person himself for several months.

If you find you are too distracted to remember what you read about SRT and too distracted by voices in your head and wild thoughts to run an SRT session on yourself, you can get the help you need from an experienced SRT student or a professional SRT practitioner.

9. Handling Someone Who Has been harmed by Other Spiritual Practices

There are people who have tried every imaginable spiritual and metaphysical practice before encountering SRT, and they can be in a state of overwhelm since these practices wake up entities but do not necessarily address the problem the entity is stuck in.

This leaves the entities looking for solutions and they can be so frantic that they interrupt the person constantly and interfere with SRT processing.

You will see the following pattern when you attempt to run SRT on this overwhelmed person: They will spot an entity or cluster and will change the subject and start talking about some guru or a book they read. You will have difficulty getting them to complete any step of the SRT processing.

Ordinarily, SRT is a calm two-way conversation. When you are attempting to help someone in the overwhelmed state described here, you will find your conversation is constantly interrupted by the person expressing random thoughts and ideas that do not relate to what you are doing.

This overwhelmed person has entities who are constantly speaking for the person and interrupting each other.

He is also trying to frame your questions to fit his previous spiritual training instead of simply doing what you ask him to do.

For example, if you ask him to tell you where a particular thought is located, he may sweat and strain for many minutes with no success in locating the cluster you can see quite clearly.

When you ask him what he is doing, he will most always mention something from another practice and it could involve something about his chakras or "grounding" himself with Chi.

If you encounter someone in this kind of overwhelmed state who wants spiritual help, you will be doing them and yourself a good service if you refer them to a professional SRT counselor who can get them the exact help they need to handle their overwhelmed state.

If you cannot find a professional counselor for them, you should suggest that they find a peaceful spot where they can sit quietly and observe Nature until things calm down.

10. Handling Disturbed Animals

Today, a student and I took a look at the entities surrounding her beloved dog, Pepper.

The dog has never been mistreated but went into terror whenever someone or some animal approaches her and this has been going on for many years.

The student and I have already run SRT on entities affecting several different "third persons" with consistently excellent results.

When I suggest that we run SRT on her dog, she was completely ready to try her counseling skills on the dog's entities.

The student and I went into session and the dog seemed to be enclosed within a cluster of entities with some other entities sweeping the area in search of dangerous activities.

Further observation showed that there were two main clusters at work, one was enthusiastic and outgoing and the other was fearfully anticipating punishment.

We spoke to the enthusiastic and outgoing cluster first and commended these beings for making Pepper a happy dog at times. These beings considered themselves as her "spiritual pack mates."

They were aware of other entities instilling terror in Pepper, but could not do anything about it. We encouraged them to continue their good work and turned our attention to the cluster that was the source of terror.

This cluster consisted of three starving dogs who had been beaten to death while slinking around and scavenging for food around a dwelling. The incident took place in the early 1900s somewhere near Hawthorne, California. They were young dogs who had been abandoned and weren't being fed and were desperately trying to survive.

The home owner caught them stealing his stored food and cornered them in a confined place and beat them to death. They were terrified and he felt he had to kill them.

They had been stuck in this incident for more than a hundred years and had an unreasoning fear of anyone trying to approach them.

I got them to look at their previous existences and they remembered being coyotes and started to brighten up. Life had been fine. They had been part of a family of coyotes and there had been plenty of rodents to feed on.

When the student asked them if they would like to be coyotes again, they got very excited and they immediately rushed off. They were instantly ready to join the game of life again in coyote bodies.

Counseling animal spirits is not all that different from counseling any other kind of spirits. A spirit can be anything it wishes to be and it seem that the choice of beingness, animal or human, merely serves as a guide for activities and does not seem to limit their abilities.

These were animal spirits not in bodies and their ability to communicate was as good as most of the other beings we encounter. They had an appealing spirit of play with a short attention span and as soon as the charge lifted, they were off and running to their next adventure.

11. Handling Situations You Can't Share with Anyone

Many of us have done things that we have buried so deeply that we really cannot remember them. Usually these will require the assistance of a partner or an SRT practitioner.

For some, this situation may have happened in a recent past life, but others are haunted by something they did this lifetime which was so revolting that the barest memory will make them cringe. We protect ourselves from these memories through a number of mechanisms which mask the memory and make less of it until it disappears from our memory entirely.

Life, however, presents us with new situations every day, and some of these situations will inevitably activate these old memories and bring us to our knees with shame that cannot be expunged.

SRT is the first technology that provides a solution to these shameful and completely revolting memories.

First of all, any revolting and disgusting act against nature was probably performed as the only possible solution to a problem that could not be solved otherwise. As has been written countless times, "desperate times call for desperate measures".

If you keep calm and start examining the justifications for the act, you will eventually spot the decision that compromised all that you held dear to solve some awful problem. Once this is spotted, all begins to make sense and you are freed from the regret you have been carrying for ages.

In addition, you almost never get in a desperate situation without the intervention of spiritual entities. Whenever you spot an incident where you did something so barbarous and so unnatural that it now makes you want to cringe, you were probably under the influence of some rather crazed spiritual entities. Spotting the entities and the role they played in your self-destruction will free you from the guilt you have been carrying around for so long.

Spotting what you did to attract them will further ease your mind, and eventually you will all be able to let go of the guilt and self-recrimination for what happened.

In a very few cases, you may be sufficiently skilled with SRT to spot and handle these incidents yourself. If you realize you have an incident that is impossible to confront, find a professional SRT practitioner you trust and get some counseling to free you from its effects.

Whenever you spot an incident where you did something so barbarous and so unnatural that it now makes you cringe, you were probably under the influence of some rather crazed spiritual entities. These can be handled easily with SRT.

SRT students and practitioners are used to dealing with incidents such as these and will make the process much easier than you expect. Knowing WHY some awful deed was done and the exact source of the impulse that caused it to happen produces an amazing amount of relief and will literally give you a new lease on life.

12. Handling Entities Who Interrupt Sessions

There are times when you are working with a spiritual entity who is in the process of searching for an incident and you will have an overpowering urge to change what you are doing and look at something else entirely.

This is caused by an entity who is trying to distract you from discovering something or who is trying to make you leave things alone.

When working with a client, a distracting entity manifests itself this way: You spot an entity and, as you begin to ask it if you can help, the client says, "It's gone!" You may think the entity has blown by inspection, but the person will have no idea what happened.

This may happen once in a while without being a problem, but if your partner seems to consistently blow entities without engaging them in conversation, he is being controlled by an entity who does not want to be found.

We have discovered that people who compulsively blow charge by inspection do not engage entities in conversation and do not have lasting gains even though they get relief in every session. This is what happens in other practices where entities are actually driven off without engaging them in conversation and helping them to create new lives.

These entities continue to hang around the person who swears he has "helped" them but his behavior and abilities do not change.

Entities do not move on until you have handled the issues that caused them to lose their body and, in most cases, their sanity.

SRT, properly done, restores the entity to his earlier abilities, and he is able to operate in present time and is no longer controlled by post-hypnotic orders stemming from an extremely non-survival incident in the past.

Running a Spiritual Rescue Technology Session

If you are distracted by an entity in session, let the distracting entity know you will get to him when you have finished what you are doing.

Acknowledging an entity does not mean stopping what you are doing—it is just a way to let it know that you are aware of it and will get to it in time.

If you become aware of an entity out of session, you should acknowledge its presence.

This does not mean that you have to stop what you are doing and run SRT on the entity, just that entities who communicate freely with you are generally those who wish to become spiritual teammates or are already acting in that capacity.

A cheerful acknowledgment goes a long way toward maintaining good relationships with your entities.

Running a Spiritual Rescue Technology Session

Your quality of life is strongly influenced by the emotional state of your entities. Maintaining open communication and using good manners with your entities will keep them happy and will provide you with more benefits than you can imagine.

13. A Powerful Undercut for SRT Processing on New People or to Handle Unusual Situations

We call this "healing by inspection" and it works in a wide range of situations and can produce results that seem miraculous to the person healed.

You may encounter new people who are aware of a problem or a painful area in the body but cannot seem to perceive any spiritual beings. This process is also helpful when dealing with a casual acquaintance who complains about some physical discomfort and you can perceive that there are entities involved.

You do not mention entities at all, but get them to locate the area of discomfort and tell you how big it is and where it is located.

Once they have done this, you can then ask them if the area seems to be a particular color. They will look at it and will often mention, with great surprise, that the area is gray or even black.

If the person does not perceive a color, he probably will be able to perceive a pain, discomfort or an unpleasant emotion.

You let them know that you are both going to look into the area with the idea of healing it by making it calmer and less disturbed. Tell them to let you know if the area feels different and if the color or feeling changes.

You should look at the area yourself and intend that the beings in the area will calm down. You keep on inspecting the area and noticing any changes as they occur.

Do not speak while you are doing this except to encourage the person to keep inspecting the area and to let you know if he notices any changes.

The person may twitch and mention that the pain is moving around while you are doing this, but you should just encourage him to keep inspecting the area and intending it to heal.

Running a Spiritual Rescue Technology Session

In most cases, if the person is actually inspecting the area with a positive attitude, the pain and discomfort will begin to change within a few minutes and if you continue, the pain and discomfort may reduce completely in as little as 10 to 20 minutes.

Once the person sees that the process is producing beneficial results, he will usually be quite happy to continue the inspection as long as necessary.

Some people seem to benefit by you placing your hand on the afflicted area as this helps them focus their attention on the area and not be distracted.

You should use your judgment on this as some people are averse to being touched.

This process is a modern adaptation of the traditional "laying on of hands" which has been in use all during the history of mankind.

As a student of SRT, your awareness of the entities involved serves to reassure them that you mean no harm. You communicate reassurance and a desire to help even though you are not using SRT commands.

This process can be used without the use of words when the subject is very ill or when you wish to heal an animal. In these cases, laying your hand on the area produces excellent results.

When the subject of your healing cannot speak, it is necessary to use your spiritual perceptions to locate the troubled area and be very gentle when touching the subject's body.

You will know the process is complete when the subject relaxes, often with a quiet sigh. This occurs almost immediately after you notice the troubled area breaking up and disappearing.

You and the person you are healing may observe that entities begin speaking up as the process continues. The process has brought them up from a profound unconsciousness to a state where they are ready to communicate and ask questions.

You may keep your attention on the area, but you should feel free to run the standard SRT steps on the entities as they surface as that will produce the fastest gains possible.

Healing by Inspection is a modern adaptation of the traditional "laying on of hands" which has been used for uncounted ages.

EXAMPLES OF SPECIFIC SESSION TOPICS

Here are some session topics that you may encounter. I have included details of the handlings done so you can be prepared when they come up in session.

1. Taking Up What You Observe First

a. Descriptions

There are many topics one can take up in an SRT session, but the topic that provides immediate relief is what the person is demonstrating when you first begin the session.

For example, the client has a haggard look or a mournful look that is in great contrast to the peaceful expression he had at the end of the last session. If you fail to ask what is going on, you can miss what he is sitting in.

Alternatively a client wants to bring you up to date on what has happened since his last session or share some wins of a social nature. You may wish to get on with the session and find out what is stopping or bothering him, but you are missing the most important result of any counseling session which is getting the client to share his realizations!

Examples of Specific Session Topics

You client is handing you the prize you have been working toward for many sessions! When a client starts a session by sharing his new realizations about life, just sit there without interrupting and acknowledge him so well that he knows without a doubt that you understand his joy and what it means to him.

The most important part of any session is to get the client to have a realization and to share it with you. Each one of these will change his life.

b. Example of Handling

This client has his own business and operates under a great deal of pressure, but he usually begins a session cheerfully. On this particular day, he looked quite harried and his face looked a bit pinched.

When I asked him what was going on, he replied that there was a lack of new people coming in and people were not signing up for his services. When I asked if there was anything else going on, the client related that he felt a great deal of negativity even when there was good news.

Then he made an uncharacteristic statement, "It's always that way!" I knew it was uncharacteristic because he is usually optimistic and sees the bright side of most problems.

I got him to spot the entity responsible for the bleak mood, and we got the entity, who was named Sean, to tell us his story.

Sean had been part of a culture which allowed its people a great deal of freedom. They appeared to be a happy-go-lucky people who built things and enjoyed life. The planet was run by a being (like Gaia, the primal Greek Mother Goddess) who ran the planet for the benefit of everyone.

Aliens took over the planet and made everyone go to work. The aliens did not have many spiritual qualities and did not recognize the organization that the planetary being had created. They were aware of matter and energy only and forced the population go to work to produce those things that the planetary being had previously produced.

Examples of Specific Session Topics

Life got very difficult and if they made a mistake, they would die. Sean ended up deciding he had to be very careful. The culture became very destructive, and after a while it was completely destroyed. It appeared that most of the population was implanted and died.

This entity joined the client when the client had become visible to the spiritual world after some incredible wins gotten during his recent participation in a spiritual practice. Up until then, the client had been spiritually "invisible" with no particular abilities or spiritual qualities.

Once the entity, Sean, had a chance to separate from the incident that had made him careful, he was ready to take on life in the 21st Century. He left the client who was now feeling relaxed and optimistic about life again.

c. Suggestions for Effective Handlings

Many people go around with a fixed attitude and a fixed expression without even being aware of it. Once you start talking to them, it snaps them out of that condition and they become "social". You can bring about a great change in people if you observe them in the moments before they become social and get them to characterize the attitude they are sitting in.

Once they spot the attitude and the thoughts that go with that attitude and the location where all of this is coming from, they are ready to change something they may have never inspected before.

How many times have you seen someone with a scowl on their face and, when you ask what's wrong, they say, "Nothing! Why do you ask?" You might think their faces are just set that way, but a little investigation and use of SRT will reveal that there are entities who are holding a particular attitude in place. They have done it so often that the person doesn't even think about it or notice it any more.

If you see a non-optimum expression on the client at the beginning of an SRT session, consider taking it up if the client is willing. You may see a real change in the client's attitude toward life.

Examples of Specific Session Topics

2. Difficulty in Comprehending Something Important

a. Description

This difficulty can be very difficult to spot by oneself. It is like experiencing sporadic memory failure or random bouts of confusion regarding something one is normally quite proficient in.

Certain critical details that are important to the task at hand cannot be understood without reading it again and again, and there is great resistance from somewhere to doing this.

The client reads something and feels he has it but then cannot remember it. After reading it several more times, he grasps it but then he loses the sense of it again. Eventually he may be able to remember what he read.

This particular difficulty could be expressed as an unexpected lag between reading and understanding what was read.

b. Example of Handling

This client's particular difficulty was in interpreting a spreadsheet that **he himself** had created. We tackled the comprehension difficulty by having him read the spreadsheet while looking for an entity who was telling him he didn't need to read the spreadsheet or that it didn't matter.

He soon spotted that a cluster was reacting to his efforts to read and understand the spreadsheet. By making him confront the spreadsheet and try to read the spreadsheet while listening for responses, he picked up a sequence of comments and commands that disapproved of him using the spreadsheet.

(This is typical behavior for entities that are stuck in painful memories. The client does something in his normal activities and that action triggers an entity's painful memory. The client feels the entity's emotion and thinks it is his own.)

Once we spotted the cluster, we used SRT to break up the cluster and bring the entities to present time. We found the incident that the cluster was stuck in and discovered that it had to do with something the client did a very long time ago. The cluster had been assigned to the client as a "security device" to track him and render him ineffectual so he would not commit other destructive actions.

Examples of Specific Session Topics

We did the usual handling for clusters and entities who have infinitely long assigned tasks. We got the entities to look at why they had been assigned to this thankless task, what they had done to deserve this assignment, whether there was still anyone left at the place they were from, etc.

 ***A task can be a punishment for the being who was assigned to do it even though the task is to torment someone else.***

In this case, the task of tormenting the client was assigned to a being after he committed a harmful act on another.

In all cases, when we find what any being DID that caused him to be punished, the upset vanishes.

If you care for the being you are helping, all the details will come out, the upset will dissipate, and the being will come to present time and leave.

Once this group of entities realized that they had been assigned this task in order to get rid of them and that their contract was no longer valid, they left. (Their assignment had no expiration date and the place from which their orders had originated no longer existed.)

The client immediately experienced a new willingness to read his spreadsheet. Since this was the reason for the session, we ended off at that point.

c. Suggestions for Effective Handlings

There are many theories about lack of comprehension and many suggestions for handling an inability to study, including looking up words that are not understood and demonstrating principles and meaning of words to others to show that the words are fully understood after looking them up.

This SRT process is used when the person demonstrates a working knowledge of the material but still cannot study it and retain what is read.

A businessman in Africa found it very hard to read and write necessary reports for his own business. Getting him to spot the cluster which was bored with what he was doing cleared up his resistance to read and write reports, all in one session.

Examples of Specific Session Topics

All people are surrounded by entities who can have misunderstandings about a certain subject matter and who will resist being exposed to words they do not understand. In addition, entities can have painful memories associated with certain words or subjects, and they will oppose any effort to study those words or subjects.

Entities and clusters can get really bored by the daily activities of self-employed business people, and they will dream up all kinds of small diversions to get the person to change what they are doing.

One could conceivably spend time clearing up an entity's misunderstandings, but I have found it more expedient to spot the entity or cluster and find the painful memory that the entity or cluster is stuck in. Once they are freed from the painful memory, they will no longer interfere with study activities or normal business record keeping.

3. Distractions Affecting Your Ability to Get Things Done

a. Description

Distractions are one of the most persistent problems that most people face. They can see the problem after it has occurred but are generally unable to catch the distraction while it is happening. They may stay focused for hours or days and then let up the slightest bit and find themselves veering off to do something pleasurable or even browsing the web or watching something mindless on TV.

Some of the more obvious signs of this kind of entity in action are a long pattern of starting things and never finishing them. Another sign is a person taking far too long to do ordinary tasks and never being able to stay focused for very long.

b. Example of Handling

Client: Independent Businessman

Difficulties mentioned: Client is distracted when doing normal tasks unless an extraordinary effort is made to stay focused.

Examples of Specific Session Topics

This difficulty showed up immediately when I asked what his attention was on. His attention kept shifting from one topic to another. During this time the client mentioned that he often talks to himself when he is doing things. (This is on the Additional List of Topics to Check at the end of this book.)

I asked the client to do several things in sequence: move things, look at things, and think of something.

When the client finished, I asked him if a voice was telling him to do each thing. The client could not remember.

I had the client do several more actions in the same way and to notice whether a voice was repeating the actions.

The client finally noticed that every action, including thinking, was accompanied by a voice.

I had the client repeat the above steps with different actions and told him to note where the voice was coming from.

The client spotted an entity behind his head and to his left. It was connected to a large cluster even further behind him. I had him cut the connection, and we ran SRT on the entity by finding out what

Examples of Specific Session Topics

the entity had been doing when he had been assigned the task.

The entity had been assigned to monitor and harass the client and had been doing so for a very long time.

As usual, the entity had been forced into doing the task after having been found guilty for something he hadn't done, so we pulled the string and found out what he had ignored that let him get betrayed. As soon as he spotted how he had compromised his own code of honor, he woke up and left.

The client was no longer distracted as much as before. He noticed that the voice effect was lessened also. I would expect that he has several more entities and clusters distracting him and giving him voice prompts for his every action, but he feels he can handle them on his own now.

c. Suggestions for Effective Handlings

Do not let your attention wander while handling this kind of entity as you will lose control of the session and will find excuses to stop running SRT and will end up finding a snack and reading Facebook entries.

Examples of Specific Session Topics

Using SRT in this situation is best done with a partner who will keep you on track while you locate and identify the being who is causing the distractions.

You can do this with a partner by discussing events where distractions occur until one of you spots the thought or intention that derails whatever task you were trying to do. The partner needs to pick up on the fact that you receive a thought that is contrary to what you are trying to accomplish.

Once you locate the being who is causing the mischief, you should find out if he is trying to help you or if he is simply reacting to the boring task that you are doing.

If you can find out how long the being has been with you, it may clear up some of the problems you have encountered this lifetime.

 When handling a distracting entity the SRT practitioner needs to pick up on the fact that the client has received a thought that is contrary to what he is trying to accomplish.

Once the being is communicating freely with you, waste no time in getting the incident he is stuck in and what he did to have it happen.

It may seem that his incident has nothing to do with what you are doing, but it has definitely affected the spiritual being to the point that he resists what you are trying to do, and this counter intention has affected you for as long as he has been with you.

It is quite likely that the client will have many different entities distracting him so do not expect to get a miraculous result with just one session. Keep checking with the client over time to make sure that he is not being distracted in other ways or while doing other actions. Once the client has handled a few of these distracting entities, he will be able to spot them quickly and may even be able to handle them on his own.

The difference in the client's behavior and in his efficiency will be quite noticeable once you have handled a few of these distractions. If he starts to act distracted again, immediately check for other entities interfering with his ability to complete cycles of action.

Examples of Specific Session Topics

4. Cravings for Anything

a. Description

A craving is an intense desire for some particular thing.

There can be many non-spiritual explanations for cravings, including dietary deficiencies, but when the body is fairly healthy, there still can be intense desires prompted by entities who seek a certain sensation as a solution for some long ago problem.

The desired sensation can involve food, sex, alcohol, cigarettes, drugs, or even out-of-body experiences.

A person can train himself to resist a particular sensation, but if he is exposed to the desired sensation when he is not in full control of himself, he will succumb to the craving and will compromise his integrity.

For example, a successful follower of Alcoholics Anonymous does not allow himself to be exposed to alcohol as he knows he is only one step from drinking again.

b. Example of Handling

I had one client who has been successfully receiving SRT counseling for a few months but reported that he had been drinking to excess and wondered if we could do something about this.

We spotted a few spiritual beings whose solution for life's problems was to drink and make merry whenever things got overwhelming. This had been a successful action for them for many lifetimes. They had many ways of rationalizing their drinking and did not feel it was a ruin for them.

Getting them to see that they were "dead" and had been so for many centuries brought them around to considering the advantages of getting a fresh start in life with new bodies.

c. Suggestions for Effective Handlings

If one cares to look at where intense desire to satisfy a craving originates, one will usually spot entities and clusters who have that intention and are powerless to resist it. They are like a group of your peers egging you on to do it and do it right now! They will augment their intentions with pleasurable images and sensations until your

Examples of Specific Session Topics

resistance breaks down and you indulge yourself in the sensation you crave.

 If one cares to look at where intense desire to satisfy a craving originates, one will usually spot entities and clusters who have that intention and are powerless to resist it.

Not all cravings are for physical sensation; some people want to immerse themselves in books or videos to experience the rush of emotions that comes from living some life other than their own. They want to inflow emotions as much as others desire to inflow sensations.

If you look at your own episodes of craving something, you will probably find that specific situations trigger these cravings. If you were handling these cravings with conventional therapy, you might find ways to avoid the triggering situations.

In SRT, you could let your craving for something build to the point where you have difficulty resisting it and then notice where the craving is located. You will generally find an entity or a cluster that wants something very badly and wants you to satisfy that need.

It may take more willpower than you have available to keep focused on the SRT process instead of satisfying the craving, and, if this is the case, note well the entity causing the craving and call in a partner to help handle this entity.

When you start communicating with the entity or cluster, it is helpful if you can find what the entity is doing and how long he has been associated with you. You might be surprised to find that you have had similar cravings for many lifetimes.

When you find the incident that the entity or cluster is stuck in, do not be surprised if it seems to have little to do with your particular craving. The entity's apparent craving is a solution for a problem that never got addressed. Do not concern yourself if the incident has little to do with your present time craving; just get the details of the incident and what the being or beings did that caused it to happen.

Examples of Specific Session Topics

 In SRT, you could let your craving for something build to the point where you could notice where the craving is located.

You will generally find an entity or a cluster that wants something very badly and wants you to satisfy that need.

When you reach the point where the being begins to look at the justifications for what he did, things will begin to lift and the being or beings will let go of the incident and get interested in what you are doing or in what kind of future they now have.

Do not end the process until all beings involved have no further attention on the incident, on getting even with anyone else, or on anything in their past. When they are eager to move on and explore, it is time to send them for a locational process at a beach, a peaceful mountainside, or even a shopping mall.

If you have handled the right beings, you will experience a lessening of the craving you had previously. I use the word "lessening" because

Examples of Specific Session Topics

there is often more than one being involved in creating a craving for something. Beings and clusters tend to attract each other if they have similar past experiences, and these associations can go back a very long way.

Once you have handled a being or cluster and have experienced a lessening of a craving, consider that a win and end off for the day.

Do not attempt to continue and handle all beings and clusters with similar intentions and cravings or you will get an overrun phenomenon where the beings consider that the processing has gone on too long. Once that happens, you will have upset beings to deal with and you will not enjoy the results.

If you end off when you or your entities experience relief, you will find that your entities stay happy for some time after session, and they will be eager to pick up any remaining charge or upset when the next session begins.

You may have to run many SRT sessions to completely handle cravings for some substances, especially drugs, alcohol and food. If you proceed carefully and end sessions when the entities are winning, you will find that eventually the cravings will diminish to the point where they can be completely controlled without significant effort.

At some point, you may have some realizations of your own and the cravings will vanish entirely.

It is important to realize that you will have cravings based on your past experiences and these cravings will need to be handled with SRT counseling also. In many cases, while handling entities and their cravings, the person sees similar patterns in his own life and spots the decision that led to the long pattern of seeking a particular sensation.

Our experience has been that cravings do not disappear until the client's personal cravings and his entities' cravings have been handled. The handlings must address the original problems that triggered the cravings.

5. Fear of Making the Wrong Decision

a. Description

This can be a subtle fear and has been a problem for would-be entrepreneurs, performers, and people in everyday life. It manifests itself as an inability to make decisions easily, even though plenty of data seems to be available on which to base a decision.

You should understand that entities have a great many fears that they have never been able to resolve. When an entity's fears are triggered by something you are attempting to do, you experience those fears through the phenomenon of "misownership". The entity's fears are perceived by the person and he thinks they are his fears. He is "owning" fears that are not his.

The fear of making a wrong decision usually springs from an incident which was caused by not observing signs of danger or oncoming disaster.

The incident left the entities with a lasting state of anxiety or fear but may have nothing in common with the area you are trying to make decisions about.

Examples of Specific Session Topics

 The fear of making a wrong decision usually springs from an incident which was caused by not observing signs of danger or oncoming disaster.

b. Example of Handling

A client had great difficulty making decisions about almost everything and this had bothered him for years. In this example, there were no specifics as to what was feared, just an all-pervading unease that made it almost impossible for the client to make normal business decisions.

This is just one of many handlings we have done for this kind of fear, and I want to emphasize that you should keep an open mind when you are contacting and handling the entities who are projecting this fear because the original incidents may seem to have no connection at all with the fear that the client feels.

The thought expressed by the client was fear of making a decision. It came from a cluster of four individuals—musicians—who had just finished a gig many years ago in the southern United States and who were heading for another gig when their bus apparently got lost on the way.

The bus driver stopped at a roadhouse, presumably to ask directions. The musicians sensed that something didn't feel right but stepped out of the bus anyway. They then realized that people were waiting for them. One of the musicians were shot, and the other three were beaten to death.

They were then stuffed in the trunk of a car and were driven to a deserted location where their bodies were discarded by the side of the road.

The initial action that led to the incident was someone ignoring a sign of possible danger. One of the individuals had realized that the bus driver had made a wrong turn and hadn't said anything about it to the others.

The group of entities made a decision during this incident which was, "Don't go it alone", and they were fixated on a fear of any decisions being made by the client.

Once the group spotted how they had gotten into trouble, they came unstuck from that incident and were ready for a fresh start in the 21st Century. The client experienced a big win as his misowned fear dropped away.

c. Suggestions for Effective Handlings

When someone has difficulty making decisions and keeps waffling back and forth between action and no action, try to get the thought that springs to mind during the decision-making process.

If there is no coherent thought, look for a feeling of fear or confusion in the space around the client. Once the feeling or thought is located, get in touch with the entity or cluster of entities and gently begin a conversation with the idea of helping them sort things out.

These beings will be fixated on some experience which makes them very leery of trying anything new. This experience may also make them suspicious of any efforts to help them. You need to show that you care for them and proceed with gentleness and certainty until they are willing to look at what they did to make this happen in the first place.

There may be more than one entity or cluster to handle in order to reduce this fear to manageable levels. They do not all have to be handled at once, but the prudent SRT counselor will make sure to check this topic in a subsequent session.

6. Aversions

a. Description

Aversions can exist in almost any fashion. This can include aversion to a particular line of work, to certain foods, colors, music or even literature that are normally considered pleasant or non-threatening.

 When someone has difficulty with something that should lie in his normal field of interest, you might do well by checking to see if an entity or cluster is involved.

b. Example of Handling

A professional musician who performs regularly and has an extensive repertoire of jazz and popular music selections is confused by the fact that he has never been able to study classical music even though he likes it and would like to play it.

When we began discussing the matter, he spotted an entity who was quite vehement on the subject of classical music. The entity said, "Not another lifetime of playing classical music!"

It was a single being who had composed and performed classical music for about 475 years. He had decided that he would never do that again, but here he was stuck to a musician who wanted to learn to play classical music, so he kept interfering with the musician whenever the musician studied classical music.

Once we got in communication with the being and he realized he was free to create his own future, he departed to explore the world of today.

c. *Suggestions for Effective Handlings*

When someone has difficulty with something that should lie in his normal field of interest, you would do well to suspect that an entity or cluster is involved.

The most common sign is a stubborn resistance to what the person wishes to do. Spotting where the resistance is coming from is the first step of the handling.

Examples of Specific Session Topics

Getting the being to describe the incident that causes the resistance may take some discussion, but a caring attitude will open the door to a heartfelt conversation, and the being can be freed from the compulsion or aversion with the standard steps of the SRT process.

This particular example was experienced by a musician, but there are similar aversions experienced by professionals of all kinds. Consider a doctor who has an aversion to blood or operating on children. This is the kind of situation where we would expect to see an entity or cluster at work.

If you can get the person to describe the feeling or thought that occurs when he experiences the aversion, you can then locate and handle the entities involved.

The most common sign is a stubborn resistance to what the person wishes to do. Spotting where the resistance is coming from is the first step of the handling.

Examples of Specific Session Topics

7. Being Possessed by Recently Deceased Entities

a. Description

This can be a brutal experience for the person being possessed and for the entity attempting to take over the body as well.

Recently deceased entities are those who have just had their body die under them and they can be quite disoriented. As a result, they can occasionally attempt to take over another person's body without realizing that the body is already inhabited.

A being whose body has been dead for some years is usually acclimatized to being a disembodied spiritual being and has adopted a role of observer, adviser, or even tormentor of someone who is already operating a body and playing the game of life. These beings are influencing the behavior of the person with the body every day, but this rarely assumes the level of possession as described by Stephen King in his novels where the possessed person is completely controlled by the invading entity.

People who die suddenly and without warning are thrown into a situation for which they are unprepared, and they may desperately search for another body to inhabit. When they inhabit a body under these conditions, they seem to think they can just pick up the motor controls and drive the new body like they drove the old body. It is a big shock to them and to the being who is already running the body when they both find that they are not alone.

b. Examples of Handling

Example #1 involved a SRT student in Africa who was invaded by the spirit of a young Zulu at 3 o'clock in the morning while he was asleep. Both he and the young Zulu were startled, and the SRT student lost control of his body for a period of time, during which his eyes would not focus and he kept vomiting.

The young Zulu and his wife had been in a car accident in a nearby township at 6 o'clock in the evening. The wife died immediately and the young Zulu was taken to the hospital where he died at 3 o'clock in the morning. He left the body and almost immediately ended up in the SRT student's body, which woke up the SRT student and startled both of them.

Examples of Specific Session Topics

It took the SRT student some time to get focused enough to start handling the Zulu with SRT, but he did some simple processes called locationals to orient the newly-deceased being to life in the physical universe without a body. The SRT student was trying to make the young Zulu feel less desperate about needing a friend to help him through this new experience, but the young Zulu still did not want to leave the company of the SRT student.

The police came by to see the SRT student soon afterward because the couple in the accident had papers connecting them to the SRT student through rent receipts. The SRT student had additional records which identified the couple's relatives and, as a result, word was gotten to the young Zulu's family so they could collect the young couple's bodies for a proper burial.

When the SRT student told the young Zulu that his family would be burying the bodies the next day, the entity left.

Examples of Specific Session Topics

 People who die suddenly and without warning are thrown into a situation for which they are unprepared, and they may desperately search for another body to inhabit.

Example #2 involved a young man who is so spiritually open that he attracts recently departed spirits from accident sites.

He is easily overwhelmed by these entities and does not seem to be able to resist them. After passing by an accident site, he will come home and will be talking to these recently dead people for the next few days.

He is surrounded by so many beings trying to get his attention that it is quite difficult to talk to him for more than a few minutes before one of the visiting beings takes over and starts dominating the discussion. These beings will also take over his body and control his actions and his speech from time to time.

The young man's mother is an SRT student and is training to be an SRT practitioner. She is able to directly contact and handle the entities who invade

Examples of Specific Session Topics

her son's space because she truly cares for entities and wishes to help them. The young man is not involved in the SRT process; all of the communication is directed to the entities involved, and they are happy to have someone recognize them and help them to overcome the shock of their recent deaths.

The handlings are straightforward. Once entities are contacted and the incident is described, the entities are coaxed to see what they did that caused the accident to occur. Getting the justifications for the action is quite easy, and the beings rapidly recover their interest in life and are usually ready to go pick up a new body and start anew.

The young man shows an immediate change in behavior when the entities are handled, and he becomes much calmer and more like himself. Unfortunately, we have not yet handled his propensity for attracting stray accident victims, and we have had to repeat the action of handling entities who are possessing him several times. This will probably continue until we find a way to get the young man to the point where he can study the SRT materials himself and start using them.

Examples of Specific Session Topics

c. Suggestions for Effective Handlings

When someone is possessed, they will exhibit the personality and behavior of the entity possessing them. This can make it quite difficult to process them directly, unless it is done with a great deal of understanding and caring for the beings involved.

Exorcism is a method of using sheer force of will to drive a being out of the body he is occupying. It has been done for thousands of years by different methods, but I feel it damages all of the entities involved.

SRT locates the reason the possession has occurred and gets to the truth of the matter so that all the beings involved can see their responsibility for the current situation.

Possession is an inflow resulting from a lack of attention to business or wishful thinking or even boredom. If a being is running his body properly and taking care of it, there is no sign of a vacancy. If the being running the body is trying to leave the body and fly around the world to do other things, it is like leaving the front door of your house open when you are away.

Examples of Specific Session Topics

If you are running a body and playing the game of life, taking drugs or doing astral travel is an abandonment of your responsibilities for managing your body.

There are many more beings without bodies than there are live bodies. If you have chosen to own and manage a body, you will need to defend it from those who might seek to take it over.

That is the reality of life on this planet, and you need to look after your possessions and maintain them if you wish to keep them. Your body is a possession like any other. Look after it.

Possession is an inflow resulting from a lack of attention to business or wishful thinking or even boredom. If a being is running his body properly and taking care of it, there is no sign of a vacancy. If the being running the body is trying to leave the body and fly around the world to do other things, it is like leaving the front door of your house open when you are away.

Examples of Specific Session Topics

8. Fear of Closeness to a Sexual or Marital Partner

a. Description

This can cover a wide range of emotions, from extreme shyness and distrust all the way up to outright terror of being physically intimate with a sexual partner. It is usually quite easy to spot the entity or cluster involved just by having the person discuss how they feel about the partner or the situation.

The incident the entity or cluster is stuck in may or may not have anything to do with the sexual act so you should be prepared for anything to come up when you start handling this fear.

When someone has difficulty getting close to a sexual or marital partner, look for an entity or cluster that is reacting to the closeness. Ask for the incident that is being triggered by the activity and be prepared to accept whatever the entity or cluster responds with.

97

Examples of Specific Session Topics

To give you some idea of the variety of causes for this fear of closeness, I am including two different examples for you to review.

b. Examples of Handling

Example #1 involves a distrust of men that has interfered with a young woman's relationships with men this lifetime. She is currently in a relationship with another woman and has been trying to break away with little success.

We were able to get in direct contact with one of her entities who seemed to be the main source of her distrust of men. The entity, who identified herself as Angelique, was still stuck in a brutal gang rape that had occurred many years before in England.

As we explored the reasons for her being there with the gang that night, she realized that she had expected a romantic adventure with her "bad boy" motorcycle gang boyfriend. She had very little reality on dating and what to expect from associating with bad boys except she thought it would be exciting. Her expectation was that the bad boy would love her and respect her and would turn into a caring creature.

Asking questions to see where this expectation came from revealed that Angelique had been treated as a princess by an uncle who had enticed her into sex play some years before. He brought her gifts and food and showed her lots of tenderness. When he left, he made her promise not to tell anyone in the family.

She thought going on the motorcycle with the bad boy would be more of the same thing. Instead she ended up being raped and murdered with a lasting hatred of men.

Once Angelique recognized her part in the matter, she was ready to start a new life. It remains to be seen whether there are more entities influencing the young woman Angelique was influencing.

Example #2 involved a young man who has a fear that escalates as his relationship with a woman starts getting serious. It is not the presence or the closeness of the woman that triggers the feeling; it is the prospect that they might be getting serious. He feels like his brain shuts down, and he wants to run down the hall screaming.

We located the entity, and the incident the entity was stuck in seemed to have nothing to do with sex

Examples of Specific Session Topics

or with women! The entity blew something up and he had to hide. All of his attention was on not being noticed. It was just a job, but it involved destroying a world. Somehow the police found out and he was executed.

Asking more questions revealed that he had a girlfriend whom he had unwisely confided in and she had given away his part in the destruction. He made a decision at that time never to get close to a woman again.

This had the result of allowing the young man to have casual affairs, but any time he started to develop a meaningful relationship, the entity's incident would be activated again and the young man would flee the relationship.

c. Suggestions for Effective Handlings

When someone has difficulty getting close to a sexual or marital partner, look for an entity or cluster that is reacting to the closeness. Ask for the incident that is being triggered by the activity and be prepared to accept whatever the entity or cluster responds with.

You should consider that close relationships of any kind, whether sexual or otherwise, involve four different sets of intentions and likes and dislikes. There are the two people with bodies, and there are the active entities and clusters accompanying each of the two people who are trying to create a close and satisfying relationship. These four groups provide as much opportunity for conflict as the more visible crowd of in-laws and other relatives. If you are prepared for the positive and negative interaction of entities, you will be much more likely to head off problems before they escalate.

You should consider that close relationships of any kind, whether sexual or otherwise, involve four different sets of intentions and likes and dislikes. There are the two people with bodies, and there are the active entities and clusters accompanying each of the two . These four groups provide as much opportunity for conflict as the more visible influence of in-laws and other relatives.

Examples of Specific Session Topics

9. Handling a Being Who Thinks He is You

a. Description

There are several different situations when you will encounter a spiritual being who thinks he is you.

1. The first is the simplest and is the situation where the being has felt he has been running the body and making the decisions about your life. You can usually spot him because of his upsets at all the things that are going wrong with your life and your body. He has been going through the motions of operating the body, but he has not mastered the controls for the body and his actual role is that of a back seat driver who sees trouble but cannot take action to prevent it.

2. The second situation exists when you and another being have been operating in tandem for a very long time. You have spent so many lifetimes together in this arrangement that you do not recognize you are separate beings. You have developed complementary skills to handle any situation and the relationship is so smooth that you are both unaware of any need to change until some SRT action reveals a difference between you regarding the outcome of some action.

3. The third situation results when you as a being create another being to carry out some task you do not wish to do. These created beings can be of almost any magnitude and capability from a stimulus-response system to watch someone or some area and generate a warning, to a self-directed being that can compute and carry out complex tasks without having the capability to reproduce or create a future, to a being of equal ability to yourself with all of the dreams and flaws that you have.

As you can see, the beings who think they are you can have a wide range of capabilities and problems. Fortunately, we do not have to invent a new version of Spiritual Rescue Technology to handle each one. The same general approach works on all of them.

b. Examples of Handling

Example #1. You spot the entity and are handling him when he originates he is "you" or he responds he is "you" when you ask his name. You merely continue running the SRT process and get the details on the incident that he is fixated on. Do not be surprised if you find you were involved in the incident also. Just keep getting details on the

Examples of Specific Session Topics

incident and any points where the entity compromised his personal integrity until he realizes who he actually is and is ready to create a new life for himself.

Example #2. This tends to show up when you ask during the SRT process when the entity joined you. There will be an incident you both remember and you need to get all of the data and any decisions that were made at the time.

You will also find that you will want to sort out different incidents in this or previous lifetimes when one of you was involved and the other wasn't.

At some point, you will be able to separate out your individual experiences and will be able to spot the times you interacted while playing separate roles.

Getting the original incident that bound you together will have the same effect as locating a cluster-making incident. The two of you made a decision that caused you to act as one from then on. Spotting that decision and the reason it was made will free you to act separately from now on.

Examples of Specific Session Topics

Example #3. This can be hard to confront as most of us do not remember when we had the capability to create another spiritual being or how we did it.

All I can tell you is that we have encountered this situation in session many times and accepting responsibility for our action of creating another being is the only way that these situations have been satisfactorily resolved. I do not know of a single instance where this has been done as a solo action, but it certainly is possible if an SRT student is sufficiently motivated and avoids any trace of self-invalidation.

I have handled this situation several times and the biggest barrier has been getting the client to actually look at what happened and avoid any self-invalidation when the being we are helping says, "You created me."

To show you how challenging this can be, here is an example from a recent session:

The client has been on my lines for many years and we have always known there was a part of his case that was not being touched by anything we have run. As we have continued to run SRT, things have been definitely opening up little by little. In this session he made an observation that in running things in session, "My stuff is always black." When I asked if that was an implant, he originated that there has always been an entity involved as long as we have been auditing and then he said, "He is me!"

He realized he had spun this entity off to be the being who set the standards for behavior. Then the client had wanted to do something the twin did not approve of and they got very angry with each other. The client had mocked this being up to be the good guy and when he was, the client got angry with him. The client said, "I created you, I can do what I want with you!"

The client punished the other "Me" by dumping all of the experiences he didn't want to remember on him. He made the other "me" a "whipping boy" by dumping all the bad memories on him and blanking out his own memories in those areas. He realized in the session that uploading all of those painful and embarrassing memories to the other being was like creating clusters on the other being.

We had to end session before everything was resolved but the client was beginning to have all sorts of realizations about his life and the long term difficulties he had with counseling of all kinds. He was ready to grapple with the problems he had created for this other being and for himself.

c. Suggestions for Effective Handlings

When someone runs into a being that says he is the person, great care must be taken not to invalidate the being or his identity. The easiest way to begin is to ask how long has the being had this identity and was there some incident when it began. If you approach this being in a caring way, the truth will emerge eventually and everyone involved will be able to take responsibility for their part in creating the situation. The bottom line is that all of these situations were the result of someone trying to "solve a problem".

This caring handling can also be used when a beings says he is GOD. If you ask in a caring way, "What problem does being GOD solve?" you will get some surprising answers and will help the being in ways you never expected.

ADDITIONAL LIST OF TOPICS TO CHECK

These are indications of unhandled or unacknowledged spiritual entities. This list is for people who have done SRT processing on many different areas and want to make sure everything else is squeaky clean. The indicators are grouped by function. They can refer to your own indicators or someone else's indicators.

This is a "hot" list in that reading it can easily restimulate entities and clusters and cause emotional and physical reactions on reading the list items.

Since the purpose of the list is to find areas to run SRT on, DO NOT CONTINUE reading after encountering the first reaction. Take up the reaction immediately and see whether it is your reaction or an entity's reaction and handle appropriately.

1. Inappropriate or Recurring Emotional Reactions, Moods or Fears

A. Any thoughts of committing suicide.

B. Feeling overwhelmed and surrounded by confusion.

Additional List of Topics to Check

C. Having disgusting thoughts that you repress and are unable to shake them off permanently.

D. Being attacked by bouts of "beautiful sadness" when reading a book or watching a movie.

E. Having incredibly detailed dreams with settings that reoccur frequently. You can wake up momentarily and the dream will resume when you go back to sleep.

F. There are things you have done in this lifetime that are so gross or embarrassing that you have never been able to share them with ANYBODY, even your most trusted counselor. You have never figured out how you could have been so stupid or debased to have done what you did. (You had help from entities!)

G. Being paranoid with no observable enemies.

H. Having questions but are too afraid to ask for fear of appearing stupid, or waiting until someone else asks so as to 'not appear stupid'.

I. Taking tremendous satisfaction in exposing a person who does not know as much as you do.

J. Insistence on being right.

Additional List of Topics to Check

K. A fixed or stuck mood level that does not resolve when addressed.

L. Recurring moods of feeling "undeserving" and "unworthy".

M. Continually whining or grumpy.

Anyone who is whiny is a possible suspect for entity action, but many of these people have their own past destructive actions and efforts to hide them being triggered so heavily that entities are just minor participants.

N. Having a Messiah Complex.

O. Having extremely destructive thoughts about someone or something and toying with various ways to kill them or utterly destroy them.

2. Distractions

A. You can't seem to finish cycles of action. You pick up the car keys and head for the garage and find yourself reading old magazines in the attic. You start to pay the bills and end up watching TV shows with no bills paid.

Additional List of Topics to Check

B. You are easily distracted. You start a sentence and lose track of where you were going with that thought.

C. You change personalities frequently.

D. You have difficulty knowing who you are. You may have a sense that you are parked somewhere watching all of this go on.

E. Interrupting yourself with non-sequitur statements or phrases during normal conversation.

F. You fidget intermittently or your body jerks and it can't be brought under control.

G. Frequently using the wrong word, such as "think" instead of "thing".

H. Having a persistent "stammer".

I. Doing and saying crazy things and then wondering where in the world that came from.

3. Compulsions

A. Talking CONSTANTLY to yourself when working on something like cooking or puttering in the shop.

B. You talk to yourself about things that you already know. Next time you find yourself saying, "OK, now pay the bills. OK, now get a sandwich. OK, I should

Additional List of Topics to Check

call that client. OK..." look around you and see who is listening or is giving you the script to say.

C. You find yourself drawn to certain people with an unbreakable sense of attraction. This is far more than simple admiration, it is a real compulsion, and you seem powerless to resist it.

D. You desire a substance and the desire is irresistible when you let down your guard. The substance could be coffee, chocolate, booze, cigarettes, and other drugs of every sort. The possibilities are endless but the manifestation is the same. You do not consider it an addiction, but your attraction gets justified and you do it for years regardless of the effect on your health.

E. Your desire for sex is so strong it interferes with your social and family commitments. You struggle with it for years and pray and whatnot with no real change in the compulsion.

F. Your sexual urges cause you to desire and do antisocial acts, no matter how hard you try to resist it.

G. Picking at body parts compulsively. This can include biting fingernails, scratching yourself habitually, picking one's nose, etc.

Additional List of Topics to Check

H. Random grimacing when there is nothing occurring in the environment.

I. Going into a hypnotic state when facing a TV screen. You will watch almost anything on the tube for hours, even if you avoid TV for the most part.

J. Songs keep repeating in your head.

K. Having a compulsion to eat certain foods.

L. Having a compulsion to do crazy things and wondering why.

M. Having a compulsion to be part of a group. Not just a desire to lead or be a member, but a compulsion so strong that it makes you subjugate other areas of your life in order to be accepted in the group.

N. Decorating the body with extensive tattoos or inserted pieces of metal or bone. Celebrating your visit to Tijuana or your first gang victory or sexual conquest may be entity-inspired or just plain youthful spirits.

Making your face into a skull or a fruit salad is a continuing compulsion, and I would expect that a brief conversation with the person doing it would reveal a number of clues that entities are running this individual.

O. Religious zeal or mania, especially where the person tries to convert others to a particular way of thinking and acting.

4. Aversions

A. Extreme reaction to perfumes or odors of any kind that others do not find repugnant.

B. Extreme reactions to certain foods when there has been no exposure to the food in this lifetime.

C. Fear of certain animals when there is no prior contact with that kind of animal.

D. Extreme fear of spiders, snakes, etc. This is not just a dislike but a fear that prevents you from dealing with them.

E. Fear of heights, of caves, of being buried when there is no history of bad experiences of that type.

F. Fear of certain types and races of people when there is no prior contact with them.

Additional List of Topics to Check

5. Physical Sensations/Pains

A. Having recurring sensations and pains that turn on and off, and this pattern continues for years— even after years of visits to doctors, chiropractors, and other medical professionals with no relief.

B. Feeling a pressure on your face that comes and goes when you have to confront something that is not pleasant.

C. While you were reading this list, an invisible force field exerted pressure on your face or head.

D. You have other physical manifestations occurring while reading this list.

E. You have persisting or recurring body problems that do not surrender to proper medical care and a healthy lifestyle.

6. Inexplicable Events, Trends or Behavior in Self or Others

A. You are a top performer in your group or your job and yet people do not seem to appreciate you or acknowledge you.

Additional List of Topics to Check

B. You get the feeling that everyone is out to get you, and your job experiences and life experiences bear this out.

C. You feel like you are operating under a curse.

D. There are people in your daily life that seem to give you grief for no reason, and you find yourself unable to deal with them although other people can do the same things and you will blast them away.

E. You keep committing harmful acts on yourself and on others.

F. A person speaking and acting in an exaggerated manner as though playing a part.

G. A person is degraded and unclean. It feels as though there is nobody home.

H. The person speaks of himself or herself in the third person.

I. Having difficulty knowing who you really are. You may have a sense that you are parked somewhere watching all of this go on.

J. A person launching into the same story again and again with no recollection that it was told before.

K. A person who is able to rattle off facts in great detail with no evidence of ever using them. The guy may be able to tell you the page and paragraph where the information is located, but does not show signs of having absorbed it for use.

7. Warnings/Messages

A. You hear your voice reading to you when you read a book. If you try to read real fast, it either stops you or loses track and you get confused.

B. When you think some casual thought like "I should take the tomatoes out of the fridge", your mental voice says the thought along with you.

C. You occasionally hear your name spoken and you are all alone with no one around.

D. When you read this list, you hear yourself or somebody making comments about the items on the list. These reactions are commonly produced by entities.

E. The phenomenon of "mind chatter" is a classic symptom of live entities "carrying on a conversation". You may not perceive this as separate voices, but you are aware that something is being said.

Additional List of Topics to Check

F. Seeing things that are not there or that are not visible to others.

G. Hearing some sort of audible noise, usually some sort of snap with nothing visible to account for the experience.

H. If you get this reaction on reading this list: This information is dangerous and must be suppressed.

I. If you get this reaction on reading this list: This group must not be allowed to...use this recklessly...benefit from this knowledge...post this information elsewhere...

J. You discover a behavior that indicates entity interference in your life and SUDDENLY feel it is not important and should be ignored.

K. If you "see" futures as random thoughts or dreams that you would NOT like to experience. Entities can and will create futures that oppose what you would create for yourself. Going into agreement with their projected images is a sure way to bring about undesirable futures.

L. Frequently thinking "What shall I do?" or "What should I do?"

Additional List of Topics to Check

8. Physical Universe Manifestations

A. Things appearing or disappearing.

B. Objects moving from one place to another.

B. Spontaneous disruption of communications, especially Skype. This is the familiar Poltergeist phenomena.

C. Things breaking unexpectedly at a moment of crisis.

D. Pictures falling off walls at the exact moment when bad news occurs.

Additional Notes

What happens when you actually understand this list and catch yourself doing one of them is that you realize, "That's an entity!"

Spotting that an entity is involved puts you in charge. You can let the entity do things for you but you will be more at cause.

Acknowledging an entity while he is at work can snap him out of the pattern he is stuck in.

The entity is saying, "Oh, my! I must stop him from doing that and changing everything!" And you say, "I got that!" " Thank you!" …..and there is this burst

Additional List of Topics to Check

of surprise and your entity may just wake up and get out of there in a hurry. If he doesn't leave, he will be much more likely to initiate a conversation with you.

If you see someone else doing any of the 70 odd things in the previous list, you may realize how much of other people's lives are run by entities.

If any of these points listed above indicated to you, see if you can get in communication with the entities involved. A short session of Spiritual Rescue Technology and you and your entities will both feel much better.

Many entities are simply trying to create any effect at all as proof to themselves that they exist. Our experience has been that spotting entities and acknowledging their presence (without acknowledging their disruptive action) is sufficient to bring them the reassurance they are seeking.

Sometimes just acknowledging an entity who is acting up is enough to bring calm and stability. Some are merely looking for some validation.

In interpersonal relationships, harmony and cooperation can be significantly enhanced by spotting and silently acknowledging the "hidden" entities that are making your relationship something less than optimum.

As you explore the world of entities and our relationship with them, you may realize that living is not all about us but includes the entities who are associated with us in a vast network of interconnectedness and co-creativity.

The real test of any of these indicators is whether pulling the string with some friendly communication reveals active entity control of the person.

 As you explore the world of entities and your relationship with them, you may realize that life is not just about you but includes the entities who are associated with you in a vast network of interconnectedness and co-creativity.

EXTENDED SPIRITUAL RESCUE TECHNOLOGY

Spiritual Rescue Technology is constantly evolving as more situations are encountered and more session results are evaluated. SRT is a powerful tool for solving all kinds of personal and social problems because it enables us to communicate with beings whose experience spans many different civilizations.

Once you realize the power of entities to affect the course of history, you begin to gain insights as to the real cause of wars and the breakdown of civilizations.

SRT is also a tool that can be easily expanded to make the detection and handling of damaged entities far more efficient once the initial cleanup has been done.

In the beginning, it is only necessary to look for negative intentions and you will find all of the entities you can handle for many months.

After you have picked up all of the easily spotted entities, there are prepared lists that can be checked to uncover destructive entities which will never be awakened in the normal course of events.

These lists have been developed by many other organizations, and running them SRT-style will uncover spiritual barriers that have been in place for many lifetimes. The results are quite spectacular.

We have been researching the use of SRT on the living units of the body since every cell contains an individual amount of life force. We have also been researching the use of SRT on life force itself with some interesting results. You can find the session reports on:

http://srtforum.info

So far, this book has been focused on the rehabilitation of destructive and damaged entities, but this is only the tiniest tip of what can be accomplished by creating a team of supportive entities to assist you in your daily life.

If you can stretch your wits around the concept of man as a being running a body with the aid of thousands of helpful other beings who perform a multitude of tasks simultaneously, you can get a glimmer of how much power that brings to the person harnessing the computational abilities of such a company of beings.

Once you realize the power of entities to affect the course of history, you may begin to gain insights as to the real cause of wars and the breakdown of civilizations.

1. Use of Processes and Lists Developed by Others

Basic SRT uses a conversational approach and a simple set of steps to discover areas of turmoil and handle the entities causing the turmoil.

Other organizations have developed lists of questions designed to uncover all sorts of aberrations and insanities, and these lists are almost always used on the person running the body in an effort to discover the root causes of the problem.

We encourage the use of the lists in the conversational SRT style where the question is asked in this format: Are you or any of your entities upset? Have you or your entities ever denied yourself an opportunity?

The use of a list in this way ensures that whoever has charge on the question will have a chance to respond. There are many lists available and you will find them discussed on the Independent Spiritual Technology Forum in areas devoted to alternative spiritual technologies. http://srtforum.info

The purpose for using these lists is to provide an organized way to deal with problems that may not have surfaced yet and thus will not be found when asking what the client's attention is on.

2. Working with Spiritual Teammates

All through history, there have been people training themselves to achieve spiritual and physical abilities that far exceed those assigned to most mortals.

Most of these efforts require years of dedicated work to produce visible results. SRT provides a tool where any dedicated student can remove barriers to their success and enhance their ability to create a viable future while leading an ordinary life and supporting their family.

The entities who surround you and influence you consist of helpful beings as well as the disturbed beings who need rescuing from past incidents. We refer to these helpful beings as Spiritual Teammates because they act on your behalf and provide encouragement and information when you need it.

Recruiting and organizing entities to become an effective organization of Spiritual Teammates is the process whereby any student of SRT can become a powerhouse of creative activity and ensure themselves of a stable and prosperous future.

First you handle the entities who are not contributing to your success in life and then you recruit as many helpful entities as you can to assist you in achieving your dreams.

The organization of spiritual beings into an efficient company of entities is still in its infancy. There is not much written about organizing invisible beings who can communicate instantly and are capable of remote sensing of information and massively parallel computation.

As you may surmise, top down management might not be the most effective way to harness the power of these individuals. Those who are working with a company of aligned entities find that things happen rather rapidly. There is much more to learn and this will be covered in future SRT volumes.

Extended Spiritual Rescue Technology

Recruiting and organizing entities to become an effective organization of Spiritual Teammates is the process whereby any student of SRT can become a powerhouse of creative activity and ensure themselves of a stable and prosperous future.

There is a great deal to be learned about managing Spiritual Teammates. About all that we know for certain right now is that failure to acknowledge and manage the vast number of beings that surround us and are interested in us leads to non-optimum situations.

Those who are researching the recruiting and organizing of helpful spiritual entities report favorably on the abilities of Spiritual Teammates to provide helpful services. They have been doing everything from keeping track of possessions and relatives to generating new business by locating prospective customers who want a particular kind of service.

SPIRITUAL COUNSELOR'S CODE

I hereby promise as a Spiritual Rescue Technology Practitioner to follow the Counselor's Code as it is written here.

1. I promise to deliver Spiritual Rescue Technology only to clients who are ready for this technology and will benefit from it.

2. I will make every effort to meet my client's expectations.

3. I will promise only those results I can reasonably expect to deliver.

4. I promise not to tell the client what he should think about his spiritual or mental state in or out of session.

5. I promise not to make less of the client's spiritual or mental state or gains in or out of session.

6. I promise to keep all counseling appointments once made.

7. I promise not to process a client who has not had sufficient rest and who is physically tired.

8. I promise not to process a client who is improperly fed or hungry.

9. I promise never to abandon a client in session.

Spiritual Counselor's Code

10. I promise never to get angry with a client in session.

11. I promise to run every major spiritual counseling action to a satisfactory resolution.

12. I promise to recognize the importance of the client and his spiritual entities in session and in all my dealings with him.

13. I promise not to enter comments, expressions or any disturbance into a session that could distract a client or his spiritual entities from addressing their spiritual or mental concerns.

14. I promise to accept whatever the client or his spiritual entities say without expressing doubt or trying to get them to change their statements to something I can accept. When the client or his entities originate a realization or answer a question, I will acknowledge that I have heard it and acknowledge it without altering it in any way.

15. I promise never to use the secrets of a client divulged in or out of session for any purpose other than to apply the correct process for achieving spiritual gain.

16. I promise not to advocate spiritual counseling as a cure for illness or insanity, knowing well that

Spiritual Counselor's Code

mitigation is possible only if the client truly wants to get well and is willing to accept spiritual assistance and is willing to accept the spiritual assistance as complementary to any existing medical treatment they may be receiving.

17. I promise to safeguard the ethical use and practice of Spiritual Rescue Technology.

This Counselor's Code is an integral part of every Spiritual Rescue Technology counseling agreement.

Adherence to the Counselor's Code is completely voluntary, but it should be carefully noted that any deviation from the Code will lessen the gains to be enjoyed by clients and may damage the reputation of the SRT counselor.

Successful practitioners follow the code and enjoy continuing prosperity.

ACKNOWLEDGMENTS

This book could not have been produced without the many hours of inspired editing by Katherine Elliott and the meticulous proofreading of Nolan Cage. Writing a book while running a full time counseling practice requires the support of a dedicated team and I was very fortunate to have these two people to rely on.

I am also extremely grateful for the continuing support of my students and clients. Their successes and suggestions for extending the technology have been invaluable.

Their encouragement was the motivating factor in my deciding to write the SRT books. Their comments and suggestions can be found all through the forum dedicated to sharing SRT results. You will see that almost every topic in this book began on this forum: http://srtforum.info

ABOUT THE AUTHOR

David St. Lawrence lives in a small mountain town in Southwest Virginia with his wife Gretchen.

He manages a worldwide personal and business counseling practice using the techniques described in this book.

David spent 48 years in high tech industries as a designer, executive, and consultant, and he observed that most business problems occurred because of personal and spiritual factors affecting management personnel and their ability to make sound decisions.

Upon entering post-corporate life, he started researching in earnest for the basic factors underlying a person's inability to make rational decisions under stressful circumstances, and this research culminated in the development of Spiritual Rescue Technology.

You can reach David for questions, interviews and counseling suggestions at

                david.stlawrence@gmail.com

Made in the USA
Las Vegas, NV
09 April 2022